M000014298

Advance Praise for
Generation Z Quick Guide
To Leaving Home

'Teetering on the verge of adulthood, the pensive process of moving from one part of your life to the beginning of another is an often vulnerable and deeply personal experience. The authors of this book fill this passion project with benevolence and perspicacity as they articulate prose with eye opening optimism."
-**Ian McKinstry,** BS, Generation Z

'As a college writing instructor who counts Generation Z among my students, I consider this guide required reading of the best sort: straight from the source and in bite-sized chunks. Most young people at the precipice (Should I stay, or should I go?) have read or heard this advice before, but not in such a compassionate, well-organized, approachable style. I recommend it to all the obvious candidates—particularly the worriers among us, those who just need a bit more detail—as well as any parents, teachers, and loved ones who may not realize the courage required to take that next leap."
-**Sue Greenberg,** BA, Senior Lecturer, San Diego State University

'Generation Z Quick Guide to Leaving Home offers informative tips about moving out for the first time. As

a Generation Z immigrant, I never had the opportunity to leave home on my own, however I am thankful to have this book to refer to when it is my time to move out as it is the perfect guide to navigate me through the process. Although this book focuses on Generation Z's first-time movers, it is a helpful guide for all age groups and even individuals who are familiar with moving because Denise, Diana & Dr. Wisdom cover a variety of topics that one might fail to consider when moving."
-**Mariam Kachi**, BS, Generation Z

"As a Professor of Psychology, I am aware that leaving home for the first time to attend a college or university is one of the most exciting times in one's life. Even with all of the excitement and anticipation, I understand that this period of transition is also a stressful and challenging time for undergraduate students. This book represents a highly informative and helpful resource to help Generation Z students navigate their first step toward independence as they leave home and begin their journey at a college or university."
-**Paul Gilbert**, PhD, Professor and Chair, San Diego state University

"While there's a lot of advice already out there on how to have a successful move, keeping it all in your head amidst a chaotic event is hard for young people (and anyone really). The Gen Z Guide to Leaving Home keeps all the advice together for you while offering

insights you may have forgotten about or just needed a refresher on."
-**Nora Del Rosario,** BS, Generation Z

"As a Millennial, leaving home wasn't that long ago for me. I remember the challenges and excitement as I completely changed my whole life and began my journey into adulthood. I work with Generation Z young adults and frequently see them struggle with both logistical and emotional challenges when making the huge life change of leaving home. Generation Z Quick Guide to Leaving Home points out key steps necessary to think through before, during, and after the moving process in an easy-to-read format that motivates and empowers young people. Gen Z'ers, whether you are overwhelmed or excited by this new chapter in your life (or both!), this book can help you in your journey."
-**Jennifer K. Felner,** PhD, Professor, San Diego State University

GENERATION Z QUICK GUIDE TO LEAVING HOME

What No One Ever Tells You About
Planning For The Future

WINDING PATHWAY BOOKS

Denise Zorer
Diana Polus
Jennifer P. Wisdom

Published by Winding Pathway Books

WINDING PATHWAY BOOKS

ISBN (print): 978-1-954374-24-9
ISBN (e-book): 978-1-954374-07-2
Cover design by Diego G. Diaz
Photo credit: Diego G. Diaz

For more information or bulk orders, visit:
www.millennialsguides.com

Printed in the United States of America

TABLE OF CONTENTS

INTRODUCTION

There comes a point in each of our lives when it is time to move out of our childhood home and begin our adulthood. Some of us dream of this for years to come, others may fear this moment, or it may come unexpectedly. Regardless of the reason, eventually, we have to leave the nest. We have heard from our peers who have struggled with this experience all with unique perspectives, challenges, and personalities that affect this transition. It is normal to be nervous about this change and to seek advice.

We wrote this book to share with you what no one ever told us before moving out. Our goal is to help you prepare for this transition and to help you understand that you are not alone. Several of us are in Generation Z (born after 2000) who have had experiences moving away from home and to another country. One of us is a Generation X (born 1965-1980) who has left home the first time and moved many, many times since then. Whether you're a Generation Z, Millennial (born 1980-2000), Generation X, or any age, leaving home can feel overwhelming and scary. Leaving home can also be a positive experience that is challenging, exhilarating, and empowering.

In this book, we start in "Part 1. Preparing to Leave Home," by asking you to reflect on where you are right now and what you might need to do before leaving. We cover topics that we believe are essential to this transition, including what is leading you to leave home, preparing to be independent, finding your new home, saying goodbye, and goal setting.

In "Part 2. Leaving Home," we walk readers through challenges you may face at the beginning of your move. We share tips for packing and unpacking into your new home, how to deal with new roommates or living alone, and creating healthy habits. These topics are critical for the start of your journey.

In "Part 3. Settling into Your New Home," we help you figure out how to get comfortable with your new environment. We advise on challenges we faced during this transition which you may face as well. In this part, we cover topics like adapting to your new environment or being homesick. Our goal is to help guide you through these transitions so you can feel empowered.

Moving out is never easy, and we hope this book will help you with this challenge. Always remember that you are not alone! Your friends and family have most likely been through this experience in their own lives. They are there to reach out to for support. There are also strangers you have not yet mt who will be kind and helpful. Consider this book as a foundation for the journey on which you are about to embark. Leaving home in a healthy, positive, and confident way is a life experience you will never forget; leaving home will shape you in a new way.

Denise Zorer
Diana Polus
Jennifer P. Wisdom
May 2021

HOW TO USE THIS BOOK

If you've read other books in the *Millennials' Guides* series (*Millennials' Guide to Work, Millennials' Guide to Management and Leadership, Millennials' Guide to Relationships,* or *Millennials' Guide to Diversity, Equity & Inclusion*), you know how this works. These guides are not necessarily best to read cover to cover. We encourage you to review the table of contents and identify a challenge you are currently having or will experience soon. Turn to those pages to start finding a solution!

Each challenge is designed to help you think through, prepare for, and plan for the future. Each chapter includes a brief description, several different situations to think about, and significant points about the transition. Many times, you can feel more confident after trying one option. You'll see some information repeated across different chapters because they're likely to be helpful for many problems. For complex challenges, you may want to attempt several interventions at the same time.

It's important to have patience and allow time to play a role in these changes because they will not happen overnight. Not everything in this book may apply to your specific situation; take what you can and try some new things! For some, accepting change is difficult, but we hope this guide helps you ease into this next chapter of your life.

As you work through the book, you'll be slowly preparing for the transition you are about to face. Benjamin Franklin said, "By failing to prepare you are preparing to fail," and with the help of this book, you will be well prepared when you leave home. You have the power to write your story the way you want it to be told. If you aren't sure what you want in life yet, that is completely normal. It is not about the destination, it is about the journey, so enjoy the ride.

This book aims to provide support and help you think through your decisions before, during, and after you have made this transition. Also, while reading this book, you might not even have thought through some of your decisions; this book helps you approach a big life change in a confident, thoughtful way. This may be your first move, but this will not likely be your last – leaving home is just the start of your life story!

Each of you reading this book is a unique person with your unique path. We hope that this book can help you throughout this exciting yet challenging time in your life. We wish you all the best in your life ahead of you!

Part 1. Preparing to Leave Home

Challenge 1: What Led You to Leave Home?

If you are reading this book, you either decided to leave home or you are still deciding whether it's the right time. Some of you may be moving out for college, others for a job, or just decided it's time to move on. Whatever your reason, might be this guide will help you with the transition process.

1. **Think about why you're leaving.** Are you going to college, starting a new job, joining the military or the Peace Corps? Maybe things aren't going so well at home. Maybe leaving home isn't your choice. Regardless of whether you are excited, anxious, worried, afraid, relieved, sad, or any other feelings, this is a unique moment in your life. Give yourself some time to ponder how far you've come and what you're thinking and feeling, write down what's on your mind, or just consider the gravity of this moment. Whatever the reason you're leaving home, you have a unique journey ahead of you.

2. **How do you envision your new life?** Consider how you'd like your life to be different from what it is now and consider where you might be able to make those changes happen. Ideally, you will be moving to a place that is the perfect balance of comfort, close enough (to school, family, etc.) but not too far away,

the perfect size and neighborhood, and within your budget. In reality, all of those might not be possible for your first move. When you can set priorities about what is important to you, it's easier to find where you want to live. These can include: same state/different state, on-campus/off-campus, how far from work/parents/friends, house/apartment, alone/with roommates, cost, and many more. We will walk through these choices; for now, allow yourself a few moments to consider what you would like your new life to look like.

3. **Is it normal to want to leave?** Yes! In many parts of the U.S., there is a high value on independence, including children moving out of their parents' homes between 18-25 years old. In some cultures, it is expected that you live at home until you get married. Regardless of your culture, it's okay to want to leave and to feel like you want your independence. It's also okay to have conflicting feelings, such as wanting to leave and feeling sad. You may want to be sensitive to others who also have feelings about your departure, such as parents, siblings, or friends. Your feelings, however, can be whatever you want them to be.

4. **Remember that you are the author of your narrative.** Life is full of different opportunities and experiences for you to explore. As you leave home, you make decisions that will propel you forward in life. It is

useful to make decisions thoughtfully and carefully, without becoming stuck. It's a fine balance!

5. **Talk to your family and friends about your decisions, thoughts, and feelings -- when they can be supportive.** Seeking feedback from loved ones on what you're thinking, and feeling can be helpful. These are people who know you well and usually they are people who want you to succeed. Sometimes, however, people we're closest to have their own thoughts and feelings about our departure. A sibling can feel abandoned, or a parent can feel grief and loss (or excitement about an empty nest!). Seek support from people who can support you as you are processing your own experiences; help others when you can but be careful about being pulled in too much to help others process their own experiences.

6. **Review your finances before committing to a decision.** Moving to a new place can be expensive! When thinking through your decision, consider identifying your likely monthly costs, determining your estimated income (job, parental support, etc.), and saving some extra money before the move. Things will likely be a little challenging at first, but financial flexibility can help you succeed with your new life ahead.

7. **Prepare yourself emotionally to leave home.** If you aren't in a rush to leave, give yourself time to consider the changes you are making by leaving home. Walk through your room, the neighborhood, and see the

family or friends you're leaving. Remember good times and tough times. Imagine what the next stage of your life will bring. Think about what worries you most and take steps to address those worries.

8. **Research from the home you're leaving, if possible.** Sometimes it's easier to explore your options, or even make decisions before you've left the nest. Consider asking family and friends for advice on your next steps including where to live, how to transition to a new home, or what they experienced when they left home. You could also do some intense internet research into neighborhoods, amenities, or groups/clubs in the area you're moving to.

9. **Consider challenges you think you might face in this transition.** If this is your first time moving out, you will likely face many new experiences that may seem challenging. You can prepare by thinking about what you might struggle with when being away from home. What are you worried about? Is it cooking, cleaning, missing friends? What are you excited about? What are you looking forward to? Whatever these thoughts may be, take some time to think about how you can help yourself prepare for those moments. You'll be surprised by new challenges you never considered, and the more you have considered solutions, the more resilient you'll be to face anything that comes your way.

10. **Remind yourself why you are leaving home.** Moving away from home is never easy, but if you ever doubt

your decision, think about the exciting journey ahead. You are about to embark on the next chapter of your life, stay optimistic and you will go far!

See also:
Challenge 2: Preparing to Move Out and Being Independent
Challenge 3: Finding Your New Home
Challenge 5: Set Goals for Your New Journey

Challenge 2: Preparing to Move Out and Being Independent

Most people think that by the time they are 18 years old, they will be moving out from their parent's house and can survive on their own. Many times, however, young people don't consider the cost of moving out, especially what it costs to be financially independent. Some of you may be lucky to have help from your parents; others may not. For many, this is your first time being on your own and no longer can depend on your parents all the time. If you have time before you are moving out, here are some steps to help you move toward independence.

1. **Open a bank account.** Start saving money as soon as possible. A bank account will help you to save and budget more efficiently. If you haven't already, figure out how to make deposits, use online banking, and use your debit card responsibly.
2. **Get a job so you can earn money – and experience.** If you have not had a job outside of your family, it would be useful to get a job. It is a useful skill to go through the process of applying and interviewing for a job. It's also good to get some experience working with other people, completing assignments or shifts, and receiving a paycheck (or direct deposit). Once you have a regular source of income, you can also get

started on a monthly budget and ensure you put some money into savings.

3. **Start to build your credit score.** Building good credit early on can help you down the line. An easy way to start this is by obtaining a credit card. You will likely get a low spending limit to start, and you can responsibly spend a little and pay it off to build your credit. Usually, to rent an apartment you'll need a good credit score (or a co-signer if you don't have a good credit score). If you like to travel or plan to travel in the future, opening up a credit card that can earn airline points or miles might be something to consider when making your decision.

4. **Try to eliminate accumulating debt.** It's exciting when you're first on your own and have a credit card. You might be tempted to buy beyond your means and celebrate your newfound independence. Be careful, though, and stay aware of how much you are spending versus how much you can realistically pay off.

5. **Practice self-control with your money by creating a budget.** Take time out of your day once a month to evaluate your finances. Figure out a method that works best for you to track your spending and avoid unnecessary purchases. This might be the first time you are handling all of your financial decisions, which is why it is important to learn a method to help you make the right decisions. Good habits you build now will continue to help you in the future.

6. **Start investing early.** Once you are managing your income and expenses and have some emergency savings, consider opening an investment account. Do your research or find a financial advisor to help you make the best investment decisions for your future. If you are employed, your employer may have options for investment accounts.

7. **Learn to cook some basic meals before moving out.** The process of purchasing food at the grocery store for meals you like and creating those meals is not necessarily intuitive. If your family likes to cook, ask them to teach you their favorite recipes. Go grocery shopping with them and learn what to buy at the store. Observing and practicing will help you build confidence in your skills and prepare you for when you are on your own.

8. **Help out around the house where you are now to learn what it takes to run a house on your own.** If you don't already do chores, start learning what it takes. Having clean clothes means someone has to do laundry; having meals means someone has to purchase food, prepare it, and wash dishes; and being a human means you have to take out the garbage and clean up sometimes. You might as well start doing your part now. As a bonus, you will be giving your parents or roommates a little break before you leave, which they will appreciate.

9. **Save some money, just in case.** Save as much money as you can before you leave home. It's so important

to have some money to fall back on. You never know what may happen in the future, so be prepared for the unexpected. Evaluate your finances and try to leave yourself enough to get yourself back on your feet if necessary.

See also:
Challenge 1: What Led You to Leave Home?
Challenge 3: Finding Your New Home
Challenge 7: Living Alone or With New Roommates

Challenge 3: Finding Your New Home

We all know the saying "There's no place like home", but it's not always easy to find your dream home – within your budget. This challenge helps you think through what you are looking for in your new home and how to prioritize your needs and wants to find a manageable place to live.

1. **Where are you going?** Think about where you want to move before taking the step of leaving your current home. If you're moving for school, then make sure to explore the area near campus to become more familiar with it. If you are moving for other reasons, do you have the option to choose where you live? If you do, what is the best location for what you are looking to accomplish? Do you want to live somewhere that is warm all year round, or do you prefer a place that gets snow and seasons? Think about the kind of area you would like to live in and what you are looking for in a neighborhood.

2. **Consider safety issues.** Wherever you are moving, consider the safety of the neighborhood, especially if you're going to live alone. Think about what "safe" means to you. Do you want a gated community with security cameras? Are you comfortable in the area around you? If this is important to you, look into the crime rates for the area and what has been going on

in the neighborhood's local news. Depending on if you live alone or with roommates you might want to consider getting an alarm system or a camera. It is essential to feel safe in your own home.

3. **Think about your new home's relative location to where you will be going daily.** Start by looking at the areas that are close to where you need to go. If you're moving for school, you may be living on campus at first, which can make your life easier. However, you may not be on campus, so you want to keep in mind traffic and looking for parking during your commute. If you are looking for or starting a job, keep in mind the commute to work as well as other places you may like to go, such as the grocery store, the gym, and so on. Some people prefer to live very close to work/school and have a short commute; others prefer some distance so they can prepare in the morning and decompress on the way home.

4. **Explore the different neighborhoods.** If you have the opportunity to explore before you move, take a day or several to check out a few different areas. You want to be aware of the options are to help you decide what might be the best location for you. The more places you explore, the more options you will have to consider. It's a good idea to take photos and make a list of pros and cons for each neighborhood because it will help you remember when you are reflecting on what you like/don't like and want you are looking for.

5. **What kind of living space are you looking for?** You may be moving into a college dormitory, an apartment, a co-living situation, or something else. If you are going into the military or the Peace Corps, you probably won't get to choose! If you have the option to choose where to live, are you looking for an apartment or a house? It's good to know your preferences, and then you can work with them later

6. **Are you ready to live alone or are you looking for roommates?** Choosing who to live with is a challenge itself, and sometimes you might decide you're prefer to live alone. If you can afford to do so and feel you are ready, go for it! Living alone will be a great learning and growing experience. However, if you aren't ready or would rather live with someone else (or if you need to for financial reasons), consider roommates carefully. Living with someone can alter the nature of the relationship, especially living with friends or a significant other. Whoever you decide to live with, make sure there are clear boundaries and house rules. Think about your lifestyle and who would be a good match for your routines. Some things to consider are cleanliness, compatibility / friendliness, pets, noise level, drug usage, smoking, and ability to communicate when challenges arise. You want to be comfortable in your own space and picking the right roommate can play a large role in this decision.

7. **What amenities are you looking for?** Are you looking for your own room or do you need to split one? Do you want your own bathroom or are you willing to share? Do you need air-conditioning or heat? Do you want a backyard, a pool, or maybe even a balcony or patio or yard? Discuss with your roommate and/or think on your own about what you want versus what you can afford.

8. **Think about what is realistic for you financially.** Before you begin your search, you should have a budget in mind for what you are looking to spend monthly. You might find a place you love which you may think you can afford; take your time and don't rush to move in. Review your budget, and make sure you will be able to pay rent every month in addition to other expenses such as water, gas, trash, electricity, Wi-Fi/satellite, and possibly parking. In addition to these expenses, consider what you will be spending on food and leisurely activities.

9. **Consider local grocery stores and restaurants when making your decision.** Are you someone who likes to be close enough to walk to the grocery store or would you rather drive or take a bus? These are good to consider when looking for a place to live.

10. **Find out the nearest hospitals or urgent care in the area for you and any pets.** In case of emergency, it's important to be aware of where to go to get the help you need. Being close to the hospital is beneficial in these situations, especially if you have a chronic

illness or disability. Additionally, if you have pets you might want to research the closest veterinarian in the area as well.

See also:
Challenge 4: Saying Goodbye to Parents, Friends, and Loved Ones
Challenge 7: Living Alone or With New Roommates
Challenge 12: Make Your New Place Feel Like Home

Challenge 4: Saying Goodbye to Parents, Friends, and Loved Ones

Saying goodbye may be challenging for some but easier for others. Although your relationship will change in some ways when you've moved out, in most cases, it's not goodbye forever, only goodbye for now. Goodbyes do get easier but leaving home for the first time is often a challenge.

1. **Preparing yourself to say goodbye.** This step will be different for each of you, depending on how you handle goodbyes and the circumstances of leaving home. Prepare yourself for how you're going to say goodbye to each person by considering the nature of your relationship, how you'd like it to continue, and what you'd like to say to each person. You should also prepare yourself for leaving the neighborhood you are living in and reflect on your experiences.

2. **Saying goodbye to your parents.** This might be hard for you, especially if this is the first time you are living without them. Or it might be challenging because your relationship has been difficult or strained. You might want to plan a special dinner, or maybe a family going-away party, or you might want to have a low-key goodbye. Consider what you want and what they want, communicate to find something reasonable, and go forth.

3. **Saying goodbye to siblings and extended family members.** Everyone has a unique relationship with their families, so there is no right or wrong way to say goodbye. You could spend extra time with them before you go, have a special going-away event, or plan a trip with them. Consider how you want to keep in touch (by phone/video chatting or social media).

4. **Saying goodbye to friends.** Leaving your childhood friends can feel like the end of the world for some. Others of us have moved frequently and this is one more goodbye. Think about how you'd like to say goodbye to each friend and know you might not be able to say goodbye to everyone. Each friendship is unique and so will be each goodbye.

5. **Saying goodbye to your home and hometown.** Every place on earth is home to someone and holds a special place in their hearts. Your home has allowed you to grow and shape you into the person you are today. Appreciate your home for what it is, no matter where it is, what it has, or what it may be known for. Consider how you'd like to say goodbye to your home or hometown, whether a tour of your favorite places or seeing the town sign in your rear-view mirror.

6. **Saying goodbye to a workplace.** If you have a job currently, make sure you talk to them about your plans and give adequate notice that you are leaving. Some of you may be in the position to come home

for the summer and work there again, or maybe even work remotely. The only way to know is to communicate with them. Thank them for the opportunities they gave you, even if the job wasn't your favorite.

7. **Try to leave on good terms with everyone.** Before you leave, ask yourself if you're happy with the way you're leaving. If not, then try to make it right even if it's difficult. That way you'll be able to start fresh in your new place with few or no regrets.

8 **Remember this is not necessarily goodbye forever.** Saying goodbye is hard, but it doesn't have to be goodbye forever. You are likely going to return at least for a visit at some point. Talk to your family and friends about planning a trip to visit once you have settled to show them your new home. Having a date for a return visit to look forward to makes goodbyes easier for everyone.

See also:
Challenge 8: Setting Healthy Habits and Staying Optimistic About Change
Challenge 11: Feeling Homesick
Challenge 12: Make Your New Place Feel Like Home

Challenge 5: Goal-Setting for Your New Journey

When beginning this new chapter of your life, it is good to set goals for yourself to stay motivated. Goal setting is great to help you visualize the steps you need to take to achieve the life you want. Goals can be big or small, and they can include whatever you want to work towards in your life. Below are some tips to help you set these goals.

1. **Determine what your dreams are and how you will get there.** It's important to chase your dreams, and it's also helpful to identify steps you must take to achieve them. Some dreams are bigger than others and may take time before they come true. Knowing the steps will help you move in the right direction.

2. **Set personal goals that motivate you to be the best version of yourself.** You have the opportunity to grow in a new place and work on anything you want to change, such as your temper, your outlook on life, or your identity.

3. **Make SMART goals to help you achieve success with your transition.** SMART goals are Specific, Measurable, Attainable, Realistic, and Time-bound. Being able to critically think about a timeline and how you define success will help you have a clear idea of the journey ahead.

4. **Write down your plan.** Writing out your plan will help you stay on target. Try to write down step-by-step or as much as possible for you to have a clear idea of what to do next. Visualize the goal, and what it will be like to achieve it. Review your written goals periodically to reassess and recalibrate.

5. **Set deadlines for your goals.** Make a timeline to plan when you hope to achieve your goals. Create reminders in your calendar and adjust them as needed but try to stay on target. Without a deadline, you will not be as motivated to finish your work. Keep in mind that sometimes things don't always go according to plan, be flexible with your timeline if necessary. You might feel discouraged or upset, but don't let it stop you from achieving them.

6. **Tell others your goals.** Speaking your goals out loud helps you stay true to them. Telling your family and friends will make you more accountable for achieving your goals. You will feel even more motivated to accomplish them when you have others supporting you along the way.

7. **Create a space for you to post your goals to look at every day.** You do not want to forget about your goals, so make them a priority in your life. Get a bulletin board, a whiteboard, or maybe just put them on paper and tape them to your fridge so you can see them. Looking at them will be a constant reminder you are working toward them.

8. **Stay positive and stick to your goals.** You may face challenges you did not expect at the start, but it is all a part of the process. You intentionally set this goal for whatever reason you may have had at the time. Remind yourself why you set these goals and keep going.

9. **Reward yourself when you achieve your goals.** Hard work pays off and you deserve to celebrate your accomplishments! Reward yourself with your favorite restaurant, a special dessert, or other treat, whatever it is that you prefer to do in honor of your success.

10. **Set new goals once you complete your previous ones.** It is always exciting to set new goals because it means you were able to accomplish what you set your mind to originally. Hopefully, you can see you have the power as the author of your narrative and continue to stay motivated towards achieving your dreams.

See also:
Challenge 3: Finding Your New Home
Challenge 6: Packing and Staying Organized
Challenge 12: Make Your New Place Feel Like Home

Part 2. Leaving Home

Challenge 6: Packing and Staying Organized

Packing can seem intimidating at first when thinking about what you want to bring with you. Packing can also be a fun process: you could listen to some music and take a trip down memory lane. Here are some ways to make your transition a bit smoother.

1. **Clean out your belongings before you start packing.** This will help you prepare for packing, giving you a clear idea of what you have. Going through your clothes is a good place to start, after going through any objects you haven't gone through in a while. Evaluate what you want to keep at home (if that's possible), what you want to bring, and what you can get rid of.

2. **Start early.** You do not want to rush when you're packing. If you pack in an orderly way, you are going to have an easier time unpacking and getting settled. Try to start packing a month or even a few weeks early, whatever you feel is best for your situation. Every day, set a goal to pack a little at a time so you do not feel overwhelmed by the task of moving. This is just the first step in the right direction of your new journey, so start it off right.

3. **Pack the essentials only.** It is often unrealistic for you to take everything you own with you and usually isn't

necessary. Look through your things and take with you cherished items that have meaning to you and the things you truly need. Remember that you might be able to buy some things you want or need where you are moving. If you are moving to another country and traveling by air, keep in mind airplane baggage limits. Every airline has different rules and costs per bag, so make sure you are aware of the rules before arriving at the airport.

4. **Roll your clothes to optimize space.** Depending on how far you are moving, you might have to fly or ship all your belongings and have limited space. Rolling your clothes is the most efficient way to get the most into a suitcase or box. Another option is if you hang your clothes to keep your clothes on the hangers and put them in a wardrobe box or large trash bags. This way you save time folding and unpacking.

5. **Stay organized while packing.** Label boxes to make unpacking easier. Some tips are: keep electronics together, use pots as storage for kitchen supplies, and use towels and sheets as protection for fragile items. The more organized you are when you pack the more efficiently you will be able to unpack.

6. **Make a list of last-minute things to pack.** There are a handful of items you can't put away just yet, but you don't want to forget them. Make a checklist of all the things you will need in your "last in, first out" box, such as toiletries, a towel, bed sheets, blanket, and pillow. Before leaving home, double-check to

make sure you have everything you need. Remember to label this box so you'll have it handy when you get to where you're going!

7. **Put all essential paperwork in a safe place.** Make sure you have your ID, passport, social security card, insurance cards, and any other important paperwork you might need in the same place. Make sure you know where those are at all times during your move.

8. **Pack heavy and large things first.** If you are packing things in boxes, it is important to keep weight in mind. Tape boxes securely. Put the larger heavier items in first but remember to keep it light enough for you to lift.

9. **Avoid reminiscing too much.** It is natural for us to think back on memories and experiences that are attached to our belongings. However, sometimes we can get caught up in the past and don't end up getting much work done. Save time now and reminisce while you're unpacking when you have more time.

10. **Create a game plan for unpacking.** Now that you have completed the easy part, prepare for the worst. Unpacking is always time-consuming; you always think it will be done sooner than it is. By thinking out what you want to work on first and setting goals will help you in the long run. It is always a good idea to start with your bed and the kitchen. Those are two essentials to living and will give you the freedom to

unpack the rest at your own pace. Remember it is okay to ask friends and family for help if you need it.

See also:
Challenge 2: Preparing to Move Out and Being Independent
Challenge 4: Saying Goodbye to Parents, Friends, and Loved Ones
Challenge 8: Setting Healthy Habits and Staying Optimistic About Change

Challenge 7: Living Alone or With New Roommates

Deciding who to live with is a tough decision, whether it be with a friend(s), a stranger, or alone, there is no easy answer. Living with someone can truly test a relationship. Living alone can be a personal test, to see how you manage independence.

1. **If you are in the position to choose, reflect on whether you want to live alone or with a roommate(s).** Think through your decisions for each situation. If you want to live alone, consider how you can afford your space and all the things that come with it. Additionally, think about whether you feel ready to be on your own yet. Living alone can come with a lot of responsibilities that you may not realize right away. If you are thinking about a roommate or roommates, do you have a friend in mind or are you willing to live with a stranger?

2. **If you are not able to choose, keep an open mind about the situation.** You never know what it will be like until you experience it. Sometimes you can make a great friend from a living situation that you never expected, or you may learn from them. Either way, it will be an adventure!

3. **When living with friends, be mindful that living together can change your relationship.** Sometimes it

makes the friendship stronger, and other times it can destroy it completely. The result is entirely up to you both and how you handle the challenges you face.

4. **When living with friends, try to have an alternative to hanging out with your roommate all the time.** Balancing your time wisely between activities and spending time with other friends will help avoid unnecessary conflicts.

5. **When living with a stranger, make time to get to know one another.** You will learn more and more about each other every day but spend time in the beginning to establish a basic understanding of one another. This will help you feel more comfortable about this new living situation.

6. **When living with roommates, keep an open line of communication.** There will be times when you do not like something your roommate did or is planning to do within the space which may cause conflict. Whether it is having people over too often, not doing the dishes, or eating your food, it's wise to address the situation before tension builds up.

7. **When living with roommates, establish household rules early on.** Whether or not you know them already or not rules are necessary to keep the peace. Setting clear expectations for household chores and sharing food is essential, as these typically cause conflict. Additionally, having a conversation on when it is and isn't okay to have guests over and for how long if they are sleeping over.

8. **When living alone, set goals on how you would like to live your new life.** Living on your own is an incredible experience to learn and grow. Remember to always look on the bright side of having your own space. You can decorate it how you want and do what you want without having to worry about anyone else. Create new healthy habits for yourself and your life. The world is your oyster, and your place is your space. So, enjoy it!

9. **When living alone, ensure that you have a support system for when you are feeling down.** It is no secret that at times you may feel alone or depressed. This is a completely natural feeling to have. The best way to overcome that is to call a friend or family member to talk to in those moments. You should also make new friends who you can go out with when you're feeling down. It is easy to get stuck home alone, but your friends can be there to help you cheer up. There's also a value to enjoy being by yourself; it's worth considering.

10 **When living alone, establish a routine for yourself.** It is important to hold yourself accountable for your responsibilities when there is no one around. Creating structure can help you achieve great success while living alone.

See also:
Challenge 2: Preparing to Move Out and Being
    Independent
Challenge 3: Finding Your New Home
Challenge 12: Make Your New Place Feel Like Home

Challenge 8: Setting Healthy Habits and Staying Optimistic About Change

When on your own, it is important to stay motivated and focused on your goals. You want to find the balance of taking care of yourself by having good hygiene, doing laundry, cooking, and cleaning while still enjoying life. Start by establishing new routines and pick up new hobbies. Change is a beautiful thing, and these changes are going to shape your life in your new home.

1. **Write out your schedule for the week.** Making a schedule for the whole week will help you stay organized and on top of your goals. It's a good habit to have a regular time weekly, such as Sunday night, to write down your plans for the week. It's also helpful to post these plans somewhere you'll see them (such as on the refrigerator), so you can review them frequently and keep yourself accountable to reach your goals.

2. **Make to-do lists.** To go deeper, every morning when you wake up, write down the important things that need to be done first on that day and leave the ones that have less priority to you at the end. Making a list of your goals for the day and crossing them off when you finish them will give you satisfaction. Try to do

this every day and see how productive you can truly be!

3. **Create a cleaning schedule.** Another good habit to start is to have a specific day each week that you decide to clean your space. If you make yourself clean every week, it will eventually become second nature. If you keep up with tasks like cleaning your floors and doing your laundry it will not be as time-consuming compared to if you only clean once a month.

4. **Try going out for a walk/exercise.** Getting some exercise at least three times, a week will help you stay healthy, be more motivated, and just be more productive throughout the day. Waking up an extra hour earlier than your usual routine to go for a walk or exercise for 30 minutes will not only make you feel better physically but also mentally because it can help clear your mind and feel refreshed.

5. **Pick up a new hobby.** Being on your own will also allow you to do the things you never thought you could do back then. Depending on where you are moving to you might be able to try new things. For example, if you have never been skiing or snowboarding but now you live in the mountains, it could be time to try it out. Other hobbies like surfing, paddle boarding, sailing, kayaking are all great. You could also begin practicing meditation because that can help you to relax and become more self-aware or read the books you've been putting off.

There are so many different options and no right or wrong answer. Don't be afraid to step out of your comfort zone and try new things.

6. **Keep busy by doing what you love.** At first, you'll be busy unpacking and getting used to the new place. However, as time goes on and you get settled, it's now up to you to decide what you want to do. You are the pilot of your own life and can do whatever it is you want or need to do, so do what you LOVE. If you don't know what you love to do yet, try new things until you find ones that bring you joy.

7. **Try not to overthink how everything will work out.** If you think about it too much, you will begin to doubt yourself and your decisions. To avoid this keep yourself busy; you won't have time to think about how everything will work out. Being on your own will help you learn a lot about yourself and that will help you grow as a person. Trust yourself and trust the process, it will all work itself out at the right time.

8. **Don't let overwhelm consume you.** The minute you realize you're going to live on your own; overwhelming thoughts will take over. Don't let that happen, instead, shifting to a more optimistic mindset, you can make your own decisions without asking anyone's permission and you made the right choice of moving out. Thinking that way will help you to not worry or become overwhelmed.

9. **Remember, you are exactly where you need to be.** You wanted this to happen for so long and finally, it

45

did. You should be proud of how far you've come so far because you are one step closer to achieving whatever it is you desire in life.

10   **You're trying your best and that's what matters.** There might be days you'll doubt yourself about being on your own, but just remember that is normal. Believe it or not, those thoughts help you realize how far you've come and will make you proud of yourself for achieving your goal of moving forward in life. You can handle whatever life throws at you, so remember that.

See also:
Challenge 5: Set Goals for Your New Journey
Challenge 9: Adjusting to a New Environment
Challenge 12: Make Your New Place Feel Like Home

Part 3. Settling In Your New Home

Challenge 9: Adjusting to a New Environment

Moving into a new home can be overwhelming. Ready or not, this is a great opportunity to start fresh by setting goals and new habits.

1. **Give yourself time to adjust.** Moving away from home can be overwhelming, stressful, and scary at times but remember that time heals all. It can take up to six months or more for you to feel comfortable in your new home. Everyone handles things differently so don't worry how long it takes.

2. **Exploring your new neighborhood.** Go online and check out what everyone on social media is saying about the place you moved to. If you have a car in this new city, go for a drive (it doesn't matter where) just to learn about the roads, the area, and the traffic. Facebook, Twitter, Instagram, and Tik Tok are all great places to reach out and get connected with people in the community to find new places to explore.

3. **Finding a job.** Some of you may be relocating for a job, in that case, you're set! It's always a good idea to walk into local retail stores or restaurants if that is what you are looking for. If not, go online, check out Google, Indeed, ZipRecruiter, Monster, Glassdoor, LinkedIn, and many other job search resources that

are available. Finally, talk to people you know, as connections are everything in this world. Let people know you're looking for work. You never know who may help you find a job when you least expect it!

4. **Finding new doctors.** The best way to find a new doctor is to contact your insurance company if you have one. Call or look online to see what doctors are in the network in your area. Some of you may currently be under your parent's health insurance, but that is often only available until age 25. If you don't have medical insurance, look into your state's options for Medicaid to find out how you can receive medical help when needed. Another option is to look into public/walk-in clinics that are available for free or reduced cost health care.

5. **Making new friends.** There are tons of ways to make new friends, but the key to all of them is putting yourself out there. Think about your interests and what you like to do for fun. Whether it be sports, the gym, yoga, surfing, paddle boarding, skiing, chess, dancing, acting, etc. there is always something that you can find in your city to do. Get in a class or join a group and talk to people! Even just going out for a drink you may find your new best friend!

6. **Discovering community resources.** Most communities have resources for information, social events, and more. If you are going to college, check out your school resources first and get familiar with what is available to you. Otherwise, research online

where your local hospital, libraries, police station, post office, and social organizations are in your new area. Most areas have a local history or park tours as well.

7. **Establish a daily or weekly routine.** Creating structure is helpful in a new environment where you have never been before. It may feel weird at first but if you stick to a structure, eventually you will feel much more comfortable. Reflect on what it is you did at home that worked for you, or that didn't work and make adjustments accordingly.

8. **Go restaurant hunting and find your new favorite local spots!** Yelp and Google are great tools to help find the hottest restaurants in town. Check the ratings and reviews before going and then see for yourself. It takes time and patience to find the right place, so don't be discouraged. It might be a restaurant or a coffee shop. Whatever you're looking for you can find it!

9. **Look into what events are going on locally for you to experience.** There are tons of different websites and resources depending on what you're looking to do. The internet is your best friend in this situation, the possibilities are endless. Look into local newspaper websites in their events section or research local venues that host events. You never know what you may find.

10. **Remember to keep in touch with family and friends back home as you prefer.** Moving to a new place is

always exciting ... and you may get lost at times. Sometimes people like to immerse themselves in their new home and don't stay in touch. Others have trouble moving ahead in their new place because they're still tethered to the past. Similarly, sometimes your family and friends back home are eager to hear your adventures, and other times they're ... not so eager. Decide how you'd like to stay connected and make it a habit.

See also:
Challenge 5: Set Goals for Your New Journey
Challenge 10: Updating Your Change of Address
Challenge 12: Make Your New Place Feel Like Home

Challenge 10: Adulting Basics: Bills, Taxes, Insurance, and More

When moving for the first time there are a few things that will probably be new to you like paying bills, getting insurance, and filing taxes. You may need to update your address. You may need to update your driver's license and insurance – or you may want to wait. Take what you need from this chapter right now and hold on to the rest for later.

1. **Setting up your water, gas, internet, cable, and electricity.** Every living space has a different way of paying water, gas, and electricity bills. Some places even charge you a trash fee. Find out from your property manager/landlord/landlady how those services are provided and paid for. The Internet might be important to get right away because you might need it for school or work. Make sure you have reliable Wi-Fi that works well for you to be able to work from home if needed.

2. **Paying rent and other bills.** Monthly bills will eventually become a habit; however, at first, it may be a conscious effort for you to remember them. The best way to avoid missing payments is to set up automatic billing for anything you can. That way you do not have to stress over remembering bills all the time. However, make sure to keep an eye on your

bank account to make sure you have enough money to pay them!

3. **Filing taxes.** Now that you're on your own, it's your responsibility to do and update your taxes yearly. Moreover, it might be helpful to you if you mark the tax due date on your calendar and have a reminder a month before, so that way you won't forget about them or won't leave them until the last minute. There are lots of places to get help for filing taxes, including libraries, private services that do tax filing, and the Internal Revenue Service hotlines.

4. **Updating your address.** If you are looking to change your address officially, you can go to the post office or fill out a form online. This will ensure the post office redirects all your mail to your new address. Make sure you remember to tell your family and friends your new address as well. In addition, you may want to update your driver's license with your new address. If you have moved to a new state, changing your license can help you establish residency as well.

5. **Health Insurance.** Thanks to the Affordable Care Act, most medical insurance plans allow you to stay under your parents' coverage until you are 25. Whether you stay on your parents' plan, get insurance through school or work, or go without insurance, it's important to think in advance how you can manage medical problems. Every plan has different polices; there may be co-pays (a bill you pay

at the time of service), preferred/allowed providers (which limits what insurance will cover if you go to an out of network provider), or deductibles (a certain amount you have to pay out-of-pocket before insurance will cover expenses). Learn about your insurance so you can be prepared in case of an emergency. If you do not have health insurance, or do not plan on getting any, research alternative options such as a public clinic, school clinic, or state public health assistance.

6. **Renters' and Home Insurance.** Considering this is your first move, you will most likely rent the place you are looking to live in. Many rental apartments require the tenant to obtain renters' insurance. It is a good idea to get renters' insurance to protect your property just in case there's fire, theft, or flood that damages your property. If you are buying a house or condominium, you should get home insurance.

7. **Cars and Insurance.** For those of you who already have a car and insurance, you might want to register your car in the new state you live in and get new license plates. Many states require you to register within 30 or 60 days of changing residency to the new state, but there may be exceptions for students or military. For those who haven't left the state then you have nothing to worry about right now, but you might in the future. Car insurance rates vary by your residence location, your age, and other factors. Until you turn 25, you will have a higher insurance rate due

to being an "inexperienced driver." If you don't have a car, think about if getting a car is affordable or necessary for your situation, evaluate other transportation options such as subway, rail, or bus, and see what's best for you. If you decide to buy or lease a car make sure the insurance and registration match. There are so many options when it comes to car shopping so take your time, do your research, and try not to get swindled by car dealerships.

8. **Opening a new bank account or credit card.** Depending on where you're moving and what bank you have, you may need to open a new bank account. You also may want to open your own if your previous one is linked to your parents. Whatever the reason is, check out the area where you're planning to move and see what banks are in the area. Check on monthly fees and ask if they have special opportunities for students or military if that applies. If you already don't have a credit card, you might want to consider getting one to start building your credit score. However, make sure you are monitoring how much you spend on it, so you can pay it back completely or mostly at the end of every month.

9. **Feeding yourself.** Everyone's life is different growing up and some of you may not have ever been responsible for making dinner. Others may be more familiar with preparing a meal. However, now you are in charge of making sure you are getting the right amount of vitamins and nutrients you need in a day.

No one is going to tell you or remind you when you need to eat. If you want to learn to cook, tons of YouTube videos and websites can give step-by-step instructions on whatever you want to make. Even TikTok has simple recipes you can try. Cooking may not be for everyone, but keep in mind that eating out every night gets expensive. Some of you may be going to college where they have a meal plan in place for you, however, if not there are several meal kit companies that you can look into if you are looking for some help. Companies like Hello Fresh, Blue Apron, and Home Chef could be a good fit for you. These meals provide measured ingredients and recipes to help you save time and avoid wasting money at the grocery store on food that ends up getting thrown out. Find what works for you and your lifestyle.

10. **Working for the first time or a new job.** For some, this may be your first time looking for a job. If it's not, you are familiar with this process. Think about applying to places you would like to work at or places you feel your skills would be best in. Put together a resume of your skills and any related experience you may have before applying. You need to ask yourself if you want to work full-time or part-time if you're going to school. Furthermore, if you have moved for a job, you should notify them when you are ready to start working.

See also:
Challenge 9: Adjusting to a New Environment
Challenge 11: Feeling Homesick
Challenge 12: Make Your New Place Feel Like Home

Challenge 11: Feeling Homesick

When leaving home for the first time, you may not know what it feels like to miss home. However, most people get homesick from time to time – and that's okay! Here are some ways we found that can help cope with homesickness.

1. **Acknowledge your feelings but don't let them control you.** Feeling homesick is completely natural, and your feelings are valid. Remember that this is only a temporary feeling. Accept and appreciate the way you are feeling. You are most likely feeling this way because you love where you come from and the people that surround you, which is beautiful. You are only human.

2. **Call your parents, siblings, friends, and missed loved ones.** The best thing to do when you miss home is to talk to the people that are home. Your parents or siblings are likely the ones who will understand what you are feeling the most. Give them a call and see how everything is going on at home, maybe even video chat to feel closer to them. Do this every once in a while, but make sure you're not spending all of your time talking to them instead of working towards your goals.

3. **Get out of the house and keep busy.** You may be feeling down right now because you were used to

your old environment. The best way to overcome this is to immerse yourself in your new environment. It may sound scary at first, but it will begin to feel like home if you find comfort in your new surroundings. Find something fun to do around you; whether it be exploring, shopping, or reaching out to friends and seeing what they are doing, just get active!

4. **Bring or buy something that reminds you of home.** Bringing something that reminds you of home can be a great way to help with the adjustment. Every time you see it you will think of home and the feelings that come with it. If you can't bring the actual thing, sometimes buying something that reminds you of homework as well. Small things like a coffee machine or towels maybe even some decorations can make you feel right at home.

5. **Remind yourself why you began this new journey.** You may feel lost from time to time, wondering what it is you are doing in this new place. Remember when you started this journey there was a reason you decided to tackle this challenge. Sometimes all it takes is remembering to get yourself back on track. Look at the goals you set earlier and make sure you are still working towards them.

6. **Establish new traditions or routines.** Once you are settled in your new home and surroundings you will find a natural groove. Establishing a routine of any kind, whether it be weekly, monthly, or yearly will give you something to look forward to. You can

gather your friends for a monthly night out or a home BBQ. Holidays like Memorial Day or Independence Day are fun days to plan for each year which can help create a sense of home in a new environment.

7. **Keep a journal.** Sometimes we do not always feel comfortable sharing what we are going through. We can get stuck in our heads if we are feeling down but writing out feelings can be helpful.

8. **Ask for help if you need it.** You should never be afraid to ask for help, especially from your family or from professional support. You could ask a friend, someone at work or school, or reach out to someone you trust in the community, such as a physician or therapist. Everyone has a unique situation and may not be able to rely on their family, but there is always someone who can help.

9. **Think about planning a trip home.** Depending on your situation, going home may be just what you need to feel better. However, sometimes it's the last thing you want to do. Going home may trigger emotions you did not expect, both good and bad. Think about why you may be feeling homesick and if this is a good solution for you. Talk to your family and family to see if they think this is a good idea as well.

10. **It's okay to move back home.** Life is full of unexpected things, and you may decide that this new place is not for you. Many people try exploring new places and realize they were happy right where they

started, and that is okay! Don't be afraid to go home if you feel this new journey isn't what is best for you.

See also:
Challenge 4: Saying Goodbye to Parents, Friends, and Loved Ones
Challenge 8: Setting Healthy Habits and Staying Optimistic About Change
Challenge 12: Make Your New Place Feel Like Home

Challenge 12: Make Your New Place Feel Like Home

One of the best parts of moving is getting to decorate your new space and make it your home. You can make your new space look and feel however you desire. Here are some suggestions to help you with this task.

1. **Stay organized from the start.** There is nothing better than coming home to a well-organized space without clutter or mess. Try your best to maintain your organizational skills from the day you move in. This is easier said than done; however, if you properly organize and label everything, you can do it!
2. **Keep it clean.** Pick a day in the week for cleaning because it will help you establish a routine, and it will eventually become a habit. Setting good cleaning habits for washing dishes and doing laundry will help you feel comfortable in your space. Remember to clean out your fridge at least once a month if not more. A tip to help keep your floors clean is to have guests remove their shoes when coming over; also, you can have a pair of house shoes for yourself if you would like. Treat your new place as your "forever home" and that will help you prioritize cleaning it.
3. **Hang up pictures and art.** Seeing a familiar face is always comforting. Try putting up pictures of family and friends so you can look back and remember the

good times. Or purchase or find art that has images of your dreams (such as cityscapes or nature pictures of places you'd like to visit). Make your space how you want it.

4. **Bring something from home.** You may have something you cherish from childhood, maybe a favorite blanket, piece of art, or coffee mug. It can be anything special to you that will comfort you to have when you're feeling down. Sometimes buying an item that reminds you of something from home can work as well.

5. **Go grocery shopping and make a home-cooked meal.** Instead of eating out all the time, it is more affordable and beneficial to cook at home. You would be able to control exactly what is going into your body to stay healthy. You should try to go food shopping once a week and have your meal ideas in mind before going to the store. Planning your meals out ahead of time will save you time at the grocery store and the stress of deciding what to eat every day.

6. **Make it cozy.** The place you call home should be a space you are always proud of and comfortable in. So, fill it with things you love and whatever makes you happy like fresh flowers on the coffee table or your collectibles in a display case. You might want to get speakers to play music to help build an atmosphere. Things like adding decorative lights, candles, and incense can help build a cozy, welcoming environment.

7. **Consider getting plants.** Filling the place with plants will help improve your mood, especially with your favorite ones. Balconies, porches, or windowsills are great places to put plants. Indoor plants help purify your air by absorbing toxins and producing oxygen. Working around plants can also help reduce stress and fatigue while also boosting creativity. Adding some green to your environment could be a small change that makes a big difference. Just don't forget to water!

8. **Consider getting a pet.** Pet cuddles can be lovely; think through all the responsibilities that come along with owning a pet before taking the plunge. Taking care of any living thing is a big responsibility, so make sure you're ready for this commitment. Cats are typically more laid back than dogs, and pets like rabbits, snakes or a reptile are less demanding pets. Making this step might help you with your transition because now you won't feel like you're on your own; you have a pet as moral support!

9. **Introduce yourself to your neighbors.** It is best to meet your neighbors as soon as you can to make a good first impression. You want to be aware of the people around you, while also helping them feel comfortable by knowing you. It's always a good idea to try to make friends with your neighbors in case of an emergency. You never know when you may need a helping hand or someone to keep an eye on your place, or when they'll need some help that you can

provide. Try to make a good first impression to start your relationship.

10   **Invite friends over once you're settled and celebrate your move.** Leaving home for the first time is a large milestone in life. Think back to when you began this journey and where you are now, appreciate the process. Now that all the hard work is done and you feel comfortable in your home, invite your new or old friends, if they are near, over to enjoy the space you created. It's your place now, which means your house, your rules. Reward yourself for a job well done and get ready for the next chapter of your life.

See also:
Challenge 8: Setting Healthy Habits and Staying Optimistic About Change
Challenge 9: Adjusting to a New Environment
Challenge 10: Adapting to New Responsibilities

ACKNOWLEDGMENTS

We would like to thank reviewers, Paul Gilbert, Gerry Vogel, Lindsay Harris, Mariam Kaci, Sue Greenburg and Jennifer Felner.

We greatly appreciate Diego G. Diaz for cover design and Lynn Potts and Cassandra Blake for interior design and administrative support.

Denise
Being asked to write this book by Dr. Jennifer Wisdom was an honor. She has been inspiring and motivational mentor to me. I am grateful for this experience to write, alongside Diana Polus and Dr. Wisdom, a book that allows us to help prepare others for their future. I would like to thank Dr. Jennifer Felner for providing me with the opportunity to intern with Dr. Wisdom and connecting me with Diana. It has been a pleasure getting to know and collaborating with Diana through this internship. I appreciate your assistance and support on this project. Finally, I wish to thank my parents and sister for always encouraging me to chase my dreams and allowing me to move across the country to do so.

Diana
There aren't enough words to express my gratitude to Dr. Jennifer Wisdom for trusting me and Denise Zorer to write this book. Being an intern for Dr. Wisdom has

taught me beyond my knowledge about life in general and I'm honored to be working under her knowledge and experiences. As an immigrant, I was always looked down on. However, being able to write this book with Denise showed me how dreams can become goals that we can achieve if we work for them. I would also like to thank Denise for working with me together in this book, and just working alongside her in this internship. Lastly, I would like to thank my parents for believing in me and for everything they've done and still do for me because they sacrificed a lot for me just to be able to get to where I want, which I'll always be grateful for.

Jennifer

I left home at 18 and have moved 27 times at last count. I was thrilled when Denise and Diana agreed to write this book to help our youngest generation coming into adulthood manage this important transition. It has been a pleasure and an honor to work with them. They are wonderful people and a credit to Generation Z.

ABOUT THE AUTHORS

Denise Zorer, BA, moved from Long Island, New York, to attend San Diego State University, pursuing her Bachelor's Degree in Psychology with a Minor in Business Management. As a student leaving home at 18, she shares insight from her experience of moving across the country. Living in California has been a dream since she was young, and she hopes to stay here to chase her next dream of working in the music industry.

Diana Polus, BA, moved to the United States when she was 16. She has a Bachelor's Degree in Psychology from San Diego State University and she is preparing for a Master's in Psychology. She is an immigrant who had to leave her home country to achieve her dreams of becoming a counselor and is delighted to share her experiences about leaving home to work toward that dream.

Jennifer Wisdom, PhD MPH ABPP is a former academician who is now an author, consultant, speaker, and principal of Wisdom Consulting. As a consultant, she helps curious, motivated, and mission-driven professionals to achieve their highest potential by identifying goals and then providing them with the roadmap and guidance to get there. Jennifer is the author of the *Millennials' Guides* series, including

Millennials' Guide to Work, Millennials' Guide to Management & Leadership, Millennials and Generation Z Guide to Voting, and *Millennials' Guide to Diversity, Equity & Inclusion.* She can be reached at www.leadwithwisdom.com.